KATHARINE McPHEE

David Seidman

rosen publishing's
rosen central

New York

To my own show-biz princess, Madison Lewis

Published in 2008 by The Rosen Publishing Group, Inc.
29 East 21st Street, New York, NY 10010

Library of Congress Cataloging-in-Publication Data

Seidman, David.
Katharine McPhee / David Seidman. — 1st ed.
    p.cm. — (Who's your Idol?)
Includes bibliographical references (p. 46) and index.
ISBN-13: 978-1-4042-1373-9 (library binding)
1. McPhee, Katharine, 1984—Juvenile literature. 2. Singers—United States—Juvenile literature. I. Title.
ML3930.M39S45 2008
782.42164092—dc22
(B)

2007037734

Manufactured in the United States of America

Contents

Introduction

Katharine McPhee waited for her cue to hit the stage of Hollywood's Kodak Theatre. After nearly a year of auditions, rehearsals, performances, praise, and criticism, she had outsung thousands of competitors and was now one of the top two performers in *American Idol's* fifth season.

In a few minutes, the season's final show would begin broadcasting to a live audience in the tens of millions. By the end, host Ryan Seacrest would announce whether or not those millions wanted McPhee to be their idol.

She was ready to find out. After all, she had been preparing for this moment practically since birth.

1

THE VOICE WITHIN: 1984-2002

On March 25, 1984, in the San Fernando Valley—a suburban area of Los Angeles—Peisha McPhee had a baby. The singer and her television-producer husband, Dan, named the girl Katharine Hope McPhee.

Katharine and her two-year-old sister, Adriana, grew up amid show business. The McPhees lived in Van Nuys, a section of the San Fernando Valley with dozens of film, video, and music companies. Dan McPhee worked on light-hearted television dramas such as *Simon and Simon* (about two brothers who track down criminals). Peisha taught singing and performed in cabarets and stage musicals.

From the start, Peisha encouraged her daughter to perform. Years later, Katharine claimed to have been singing since the age of two.

In 2007, Peisha McPhee and her daughter Katharine attend the Step Up Women's Network luncheon honoring inspirational women. Peisha is a voice teacher who has sung in nightclubs and stage musicals.

Young kids often copy older brothers or sisters. When Adriana took dance lessons at an early age, so did Katharine.

Katharine also took up acting. "I've been practicing in the mirror since I was, like, four, trying to shed a tear (and) making the faces" that actresses do on television, she said. By the age of five, she was set on a career as an entertainer.

At age seven, Katherine did her first show. She sang the upbeat "Jingle Bell Rock" during a church Christmas pageant. Not long afterward, the McPhee sisters began singing and dancing at recitals and other events.

Katharine loved entertaining, but becoming a performer can be rough when your father's a producer. After all, producers often judge, criticize, and fire performers. "I was really fearful of my father," McPhee has said. "It took years and years and years to overcome that."

As those years passed, Katharine found musical heroes, especially singers whose voices soared. She particularly liked Celine Dion—who grew famous with theme songs from movies such as *Beauty and the Beast* and *Titanic*—and the gleaming vocals of Whitney Houston.

Her favorite, though, was Mariah Carey. She admired Carey's beauty and glamorous life, and she copied her soulful soprano voice.

New Home, New Troubles

In 1996, when Katharine McPhee was twelve, her family moved a few miles south from Van Nuys to the more prosperous suburb

Mariah Carey was one of McPhee's early musical heroes. She remembers "laying on [the] carpet in the hallway with my little tape recorder, playing her songs over and over, and imitating her."

of Sherman Oaks. Around the same time, she started worrying about her body.

McPhee had always been skinny, but she developed curves as she entered her teen years. At fourteen, when she enrolled in Notre Dame High School, she looked like she was sixteen. The school's boys appreciated her figure, but she wasn't happy. "I was always like, 'I've got to lose five more pounds.'"

At the same time, she found a home in the school's drama department. She performed in musicals under Judy Weldon, an experienced theater director. Weldon pushed the students to respect their work and to behave as serious artists.

Before McPhee finished tenth grade, people were encouraging her to try her luck at acting professionally. She did a national TV commercial and a few other jobs, but not much else.

She soon quit. "I wasn't too career-oriented because I was still developing myself," she said. "I got involved in all the after-school programs and developed a love for musical theater."

McPhee's attempts at performing professionally did have one lasting effect: sharper self-criticism of her body. "Casting directors kept telling me I needed to lose ten pounds," she has said. "I was crushed."

She would exercise obsessively and skip meals all day, only to binge on food at night. "Some days I'd wake up with 'the feeling,' as I call it—overwhelmed with desperation and loneliness—and a strong urge to feed that feeling," she has said.

At age seventeen, she found a way to lose what she ate: purging, or vomiting, to keep her weight down. The cycle of bingeing and purging, called bulimia, can weaken the heart, cause pain in the intestines and stomach, and tear up the throat.

Like most bulimics, McPhee was ashamed of herself. To fight her disorder, she went to therapists and dieticians, joined Food Addicts Anonymous, and prayed for relief. Some of her efforts were successful, but not for long. She always returned to bingeing and purging.

High School Princess

No one looking at McPhee would suspect that she suffered a serious physical or emotional problem. She had plenty of boyfriends, performed in school musicals, and was a member of Notre Dame's swim team. (Although she was an athlete, she was still self-conscious about her figure. "I'd get out of the pool and really rush for the towel," she remembered.) In her senior

McPhee was a popular student at Sherman Oaks's Notre Dame High School. In May 2006, four years after she graduated, she became an *American Idol* finalist and returned to Notre Dame for a celebration in her honor.

year, she became homecoming princess and won election as student body vice president.

In addition, she was growing more and more eager to master musical theater. In July and August 2002, she attended the California State Summer School for the Arts. The four-week program, also called InnerSpark, trains teenagers in film, creative writing, visual arts, music, dance, theater, and animation.

McPhee tasted college life at InnerSpark. It takes place at California Institute for the Arts, a university for artists, performers, and filmmakers located about twenty miles (thirty-two kilometers) northwest of Sherman Oaks. InnerSpark's teenagers not only study at the campus; they also live there like real college students.

The experience probably came in handy, since McPhee would soon be at college full-time. In late 2001, she applied to the Boston Conservatory, a performing arts academy with a strong reputation for musical theater. Applying to the school required a singing, dancing, and acting audition. By the time McPhee graduated from Notre Dame in June 2002, the conservatory had accepted her.

Something else happened around that time. On June 11, a new TV series hit the air. No one expected it to become a national obsession, but it did. Its name? *American Idol*.

Chapter 2

I BELIEVE I CAN FLY: 2002–2005

The Boston Conservatory, nicknamed BoCo, is small compared to Notre Dame High School. Notre Dame has about 1,200 students; BoCo usually has fewer than 200.

As a musical theater major, Katharine McPhee took courses in subjects such as acting, history of the musical theater, movement, voice, and liberal arts (reading and writing). The workload was heavy, and teachers quickly caught anyone who was slacking off.

Plenty of teenagers living away from home for the first time gain weight. "I definitely put on the 'freshman 20,'" McPhee said years later.

Despite her workload and weight gain, she was happy. She was getting superb training for the entertainment career of her dreams.

She even had time for a little TV. "My dorm mate one floor below me was the only guy with a television in his room," she recalled. "I remember everyone crowding around and being like, 'Go, Kelly'"—cheering for Kelly Clarkson, the first *American Idol* winner. When Clarkson won the competition on September 4, 2002, McPhee watched "the confetti coming down, her crying— I remember being envious and thinking, 'How cool is that?'"

Singing for Her Summer

Boston Conservatory's school year ended in May 2003. Though the school offers summer sessions, McPhee went back to Sherman Oaks. She didn't stay long, though. In early July, she left for the Broadway Theatre Project (BTP). Founded by Broadway star and director Ann Reinking, the three-week training program auditions hundreds of young actors, singers, and dancers but accepts only 150 to 200 of them.

BTP trained McPhee and other students at the University

Ann Reinking founded the Broadway Theatre Project in 1991. It has been called "Broadway boot camp" because of the hard work that it imposes on its students.

of South Florida in Tampa. The program ended with a show called *Broadway 2003*. The young performers did a rap song based on Shakespeare's poetry, danced a disco number, sang "It's a Woman's World" from the Broadway musical *The Full Monty*, and performed other acts, some of which they had written.

The Audition Trail

McPhee returned to BoCo in autumn 2003. By then, she had acquired an agent who encouraged her to return to Los Angeles. Coming soon was the winter pilot season, when TV production companies shoot pilots (sample episodes) of new series. If a TV network likes a pilot enough to order several episodes and put them on the air, its cast members could become famous.

At the end of BoCo's fall semester, McPhee quit school, returned to her parents' house, and made the rounds of TV producers' offices.

But her agent sent her to audition for roles she didn't like, and she usually didn't get hired. McPhee blamed her weight. Casting directors liked her, but they said she was too heavy.

"I'd cry every day," McPhee recalled. "I'd tell my mom (that moving back home) was the worst decision."

Back to the Stage

Not everything was hopeless. McPhee picked up a small role in *Crazy*, a movie about a country-music star. She played one of two sisters in *You Are Here*, an unaired MTV soap-opera pilot. In summer 2004, she went back to the Broadway Theatre Project.

Her return to live musical performance may have encouraged her to aim more at theater than at the screen. After she returned to Los Angeles, she auditioned for James Mellon, a director who was mounting a revival of the popular musical *Annie Get Your Gun.* According to Kevin Bailey, who performed opposite McPhee in the play, "She came in (to audition) and blew everybody away."

Annie Get Your Gun ran from March 11 to March 20, 2005, at the Fred Kavli Theatre, about a half-hour's drive from McPhee's home. "McPhee has it all," the *Ventura County Star* newspaper gushed. "A voice fit for beguiling or bellowing, a naturally amiable presence, and fresh good looks."

Mellon hired McPhee for his next production. It was *The Ghost and Mrs. Muir,* an original musical based on a novel about a widow and the spirit of a sea captain who haunts her home. In the show, McPhee played Mrs. Muir's daughter, Anna, an aspiring actress. The play ran from May 26 through July 31, 2005, at the NoHo Arts Center in North Hollywood. The theater was less than five miles (eight km) from her home. The reviews praised the entire cast but didn't focus on McPhee.

On to *Idol*

After *The Ghost and Mrs. Muir* closed, McPhee began rehearsing a stage musical based on pop-rock songs from the 1980s. She also continued to try out for movies and TV.

Irving Berlin's
ANNIE GET YOUR GUN

McPhee and costar Kevin Bailey are pictured in this poster for *Annie Get Your Gun*. The Los Angeles Stage Alliance—an association of theaters, producers, and other supporters of live shows—nominated McPhee for its Ovation Award as best lead actress in a musical.

At the same time, *American Idol* had announced auditions for its fifth season. McPhee's friends encouraged her to try out, but she wasn't so enthusiastic. Still, in mid-August—with an attitude of "What have I got to lose?"—McPhee drove with Nick Cokas, her boyfriend, to San Francisco, where *Idol* was auditioning singers.

As the time approached for her to perform for *Idol* producer Megan Michaels, McPhee wanted to drop out. Only Cokas's urging made her stay. She was so unsure of *Idol* that she hadn't even picked a song for her audition. With less than two minutes to go, she chose "Run to You," a soaring Whitney Houston ballad about a woman yearning for a man to comfort her.

The selection was a winner, and Michaels passed McPhee on to the next level of auditions: *Idol* executive producers Nigel Lythgoe and Ken Warwick. Again, she sang "Run to You." Lythgoe and Warwick apparently appreciated McPhee's beauty as well as her talent. "They let go of some really good people and kept people who were pretty," McPhee said afterward.

Nevertheless, she was growing more determined to win. Days later, she auditioned before *Idol*'s star judges: Simon Cowell, Randy Jackson, and Paula Abdul. If she passed, she would be one of only twenty-four contestants to compete in *Idol*'s upcoming season. With her mother just outside the stage door, McPhee—otherwise known as Contestant #32342— belted out Billie Holiday's gospel-drenched "God Bless the Child" until Cowell quietly said, "OK." He added, "Parts of that were absolutely fantastic."

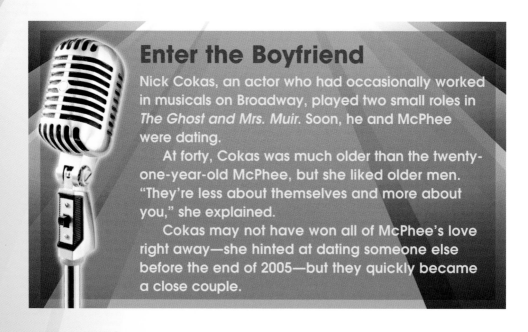

Enter the Boyfriend

Nick Cokas, an actor who had occasionally worked in musicals on Broadway, played two small roles in *The Ghost and Mrs. Muir*. Soon, he and McPhee were dating.

At forty, Cokas was much older than the twenty-one-year-old McPhee, but she liked older men. "They're less about themselves and more about you," she explained.

Cokas may not have won all of McPhee's love right away—she hinted at dating someone else before the end of 2005—but they quickly became a close couple.

"Thank you," McPhee said with a girlish giggle.

"Best voice I've heard so far this auditioning season," Jackson declared.

"Thank you," McPhee said again, on the edge of crying.

"You're absolutely beautiful, too," said Abdul. "How old are you?"

"Twenty-one," McPhee answered in a tiny voice as she held back tears.

"I'll tell you what I love about you," Cowell said. "You're very current."

"Current?" McPhee asked.

"In other words, you're on the money," Cowell explained. "It's not stage school. It's not wannabe-ish. It's just very, very, very what's happening today."

"And what a natural gift," added Jackson.

"You are sailing through to Hollywood, young lady," Cowell decreed.

McPhee exited the studio weeping and smiling, practically falling into her mother's arms. She was about to become famous.

American Idol judge Simon Cowell, host Ryan Seacrest, and judges Randy Jackson and Paula Abdul pose together after a performance in May 2006.

Battling the Beast

But McPhee had a secret problem. Bulimia still gripped her. Her frequent vomiting was, she said, like "putting a sledgehammer to your vocal cords." In late fall 2005, she checked into a clinic for people who can't manage their relationship with food: the Eating Disorder Center of California (EDCC).

She entered EDCC's intense Day Treatment Program. For three months, six days a week, from 9:00 AM to 7:00 PM, McPhee underwent psychotherapy sessions, met with doctors and dieticians, and ate meals that EDCC staff supervised. "The first day I sat down with the other girls (for a meal)," she recalled, "I cried at the table. It was just too overwhelming . . . going face-to-face and seeing the other girls struggling."

By early 2006, McPhee had learned "intuitive eating." That is, she ate only when hungry, not when anxiety or other feelings drove her to the fridge. She quit vomiting as well. By forcing her to tackle bulimia, "*American Idol* saved my life," McPhee said. She was ready to become a star.

Chapter 3

AGAINST ALL ODDS: JANUARY–MAY 2006

The producers of *Idol* housed their twenty-four top contestants near the CBS Television City studios, about a half-hour drive south of Sherman Oaks. McPhee roomed with Kellie Pickler, a teen country singer from the little town of Albemarle, North Carolina. The two became friends almost instantly.

Public Relations

The 2006 season's first seven episodes, from January 17 to February 7, featured singers' auditions. McPhee's audition aired on January 25. Most *Idol* watchers posting on the show's online forums complimented her voice and beauty. But as early as February 9 on sites like AmericanIdol.com, people were attacking her for cooing, howling, and wailing to

McPhee sings Stevie Wonder's "All in Love Is Fair" on *American Idol*. It was the first performance of hers that the *Idol* judges disliked.

indicate deep emotion and adding extra notes, syllables, and quavers to create a bluesy soulfulness. "Those *Idol* forums—like AmericanIdol.com—should be shut down," McPhee said.

Her fans came to her defense By mid-February, they had set up Web sites such as KatharineFans.com.

Idol soon began a weekly cycle: a performance show, when the singers displayed their talents; and a results show, when viewers voted by phone for their favorites. McPhee's first performance episode fell on February 21. She sang "Since I Fell for You," a torch song that Barbra Streisand had made famous. The judges liked McPhee, and on the results show two nights later, enough viewers voted for her to send her into the next round as one of the top twenty contestants.

On February 28, McPhee performed singer-songwriter Stevie Wonder's "All in Love Is Fair," a sad, soulful ballad. For the first time, the judges didn't rave over her. "You picked kind of a safe choice (of song)," Randy Jackson said. "It's just OK for me." Paula Abdul wasn't thrilled with the song, either, although she added, "You're still a star!" Simon Cowell said, "Not your best night by a mile."

March: Fighting Back

On March 2, two days after McPhee sang "All in Love Is Fair," came the results episode. The public voted four more performers off but kept McPhee.

On March 7, during the next performance show, she ripped into Aretha Franklin's feisty, exuberant "Think," a shout at a man about to lose his woman. "We got a hot one right here!" Jackson crowed. A delighted Abdul told McPhee, "It is really fun to see you have fun out there." Cowell concluded, "Once again, you're going to sail through." During the results show two days later, the audience chose McPhee as one of *Idol's* top twelve semifinalists.

The following days were tense. The producers had decreed that for the next performance show, on March 14, the performers would sing Stevie Wonder songs. "My heart kind of sunk," she said, "because I had already attempted a Stevie Wonder song, and it didn't go over so well."

McPhee chose to sing Wonder's cry of devotion "Until You Come Back to Me." To her relief, the judges approved. "Tonight," Abdul said, "was your best performance ever." The results show two nights afterward confirmed McPhee's victory. The audience voted off another singer and kept McPhee.

The next performance show, on March 21, featured songs from the 1950s. Las Vegas entertainer Barry Manilow coached

Pressure and Tears

As winter 2006 gave way to spring, McPhee began to feel the pressure of *Idol* life. Twice a week, she appeared live on TV to face judgment before millions. In between shows, she selected and learned songs; handled rehearsals, wardrobe fittings, and many other details that go into the preparation of a TV program; and posed for publicity pictures, gave interviews, and made public appearances.

Some singers lean on their fans in stressful times. The citizens of Albemarle, North Carolina, for instance, celebrated Kellie Pickler with window signs and newspaper headlines. Other contestants' hometowns poured out similar waves of admiration, but Los Angelenos were accustomed to rising young singers. They didn't cheer much for McPhee.

She might have taken comfort in her family, friends, and boyfriend, but life in the *Idol* apartments cut her off from them. The producers even hired guards to keep the contestants from spilling details about the show or misbehaving in embarrassing ways. "I definitely have crumbled under pressure," McPhee said, "and definitely have gone behind closed doors and cried and just not wanted to do it anymore."

McPhee to sing as if she were addressing just one person rather than millions. On the show, she sang the love song "Come Rain or Come Shine." While Jackson said it wasn't his favorite McPhee performance, all three judges liked her work. Cowell added, "Tonight, you turned into a star."

"Songs of the Twenty-First Century" was the theme for March 28, the next performance show. McPhee sang Christina Aguilera's inspirational "The Voice Within," a call to trust one's own feelings. The judges liked McPhee's voice but thought that she copied Aguilera's version too closely. In the voting on the results show two nights later, McPhee placed among the bottom three contestants—good enough to advance her to the next episode, but dangerously close to elimination.

April: Risk and Triumph

On April 4, the contestants sang country music, a style far from the Broadway classics and soulful pop that McPhee knew best. She consulted with country veteran Kenny Rogers and picked Nashville diva Faith Hill's "Bringing Out the Elvis." The raw, bluesy tune about rising into joy and passion wasn't traditional country, and McPhee carried it off well. Her only problem was Cowell. He declared, "That song was just so peculiar." But, he admitted, he hated country music. In any event, the voters easily approved McPhee on the results show two nights later.

Queen—a British rock group known for boastful anthems and complicated vocal arrangements—supplied the next week's songs. For the performance show on April 11, McPhee sang "Who Wants to Live Forever," an urgent plea for love. Jackson and Cowell said McPhee wasn't always in proper tune, but they liked her work overall. Abdul even compared her to Celine Dion and Barbra Streisand. The results episode on April 13 cut the number of contestants down to seven, including McPhee.

The top twelve *Idol* contestants of Season Five are photographed at a party in March 2006: *(standing)* Bucky Covington, Kellie Pickler, Paris Bennett, Lisa Tucker, Kevin Covias, Taylor Hicks, Melissa McGhee, Ace Young, Mandisa, and Katharine McPhee; *(kneeling)* Elliott Yamin and Chris Daughtry.

The next show, which covered "The Great American Songbook"—classic tunes, primarily from Broadway—fit McPhee like a warm hug. Raspy-voiced song stylist Rod Stewart helped McPhee select 1926's yearning, almost prayerful "Someone to Watch Over Me." On April 18's performance show, she was the last contestant to sing. Cowell said, "You made the others look like good amateurs," and she easily racked up votes on the results show the following night.

The next episode featured love songs. With opera star Andrea Bocelli and songwriter David Foster, McPhee rehearsed Whitney Houston's "I Have Nothing." Written by Foster, the song was a roaring demand for a lover not to leave.

On April 25, the night of the show, McPhee strode out in a blazing yellow gown with a top that showed off her curves and a skirt slit up to her hips. She seemed ready to command the night, but the judges felt that the song defeated her. "It was way too big for you," Jackson said. Cowell agreed: "By choosing that song, it is like coming out here and saying, 'I am as good as Whitney Houston.' You're not." Abdul, who usually gushed over McPhee, said her voice fell flat. Even host Ryan Seacrest, in praising McPhee's beauty, said she'd earn plenty of call-in votes "(from viewers) who don't have their volume on."

Still, McPhee was happy. For the first time, she felt truly free on *Idol*'s stage. In the next night's results show, the public eliminated her friend Kellie Pickler but gave McPhee millions of votes.

May: Burdens and Opportunities

In the next episode, on May 2, each singer had two songs—one from the year when he or she was born, and one from 2006. For the song of her birth year, McPhee picked "Against All Odds," a ballad about waiting for a lost love to return.

The judges felt she hadn't mastered the music. Jackson observed that she sang in the wrong key, and Cowell said, "The song got away from you." McPhee needed her second song to rescue her.

Folk-rocker K. T. Tunstall's "Black Horse and the Cherry Tree" is full of punchy, galloping rhythms propelling dreamlike lyrics about meeting a horse by a tree and refusing the horse's marriage proposal. McPhee, kneeling and barefoot, belted the song out. "That's more like the Katharine that I grew to love," Jackson said. The other judges agreed.

The next night, the audience voted teen R & B singer Paris Bennett off the show. McPhee was the only female left against bluesman Taylor Hicks; funk crooner Elliott Yamin; and grunge-style rocker Chris Daughtry.

Still, the judges' criticism of "Against All Odds" had shaken McPhee. Worse yet, the next performance show, on May 9, would celebrate Elvis Presley. The "King of Rock 'n' Roll" often sang rougher and faster than McPhee. Her rehearsals went poorly, and she felt defeated and inept.

On the performance show, she blasted through a combination of two straight-ahead rock shouters by Presley: "All Shook Up" and "Hound Dog." Unfortunately, she forgot some lyrics to "All Shook Up" and apparently tried to make up for the error by pushing herself too hard. "It looked like a desperate, manic audition," said Cowell.

Later came "Can't Help Falling in Love," a simple but moving confession of helpless devotion. McPhee gave the song musical fireworks, including stretched-out vowels and runs up and down the scale. Cowell criticized the performance as "over the top" and "just too much." Abdul said she preferred McPhee's other Presley songs.

During the results episode the next night, McPhee expected the audience to vote her off the show. They shocked her and millions of other people by dumping Chris Daughtry instead. *Idol* fans immediately protested. "That was hurtful," McPhee said. "(So the next week,) I came back swinging hard."

Each singer had to prepare three songs for the next show, which aired on May 16. McPhee chose jazz queen Ella Fitzgerald's "I Ain't Got Nothin' But the Blues." However, the judges felt her interpretation was no better than adequate.

Record company chief Clive Davis gave McPhee R. Kelly's passionate "I Believe I Can Fly" and helped her rehearse. She poured her flashiest vocal theatrics into the song, but the judges' reactions were mixed. Jackson complained that she shouldn't have overloaded the song with so many frills, Cowell said she did well despite a few bad notes, and Abdul didn't seem to know what to say.

Cowell chose McPhee's third song, the wistful *Wizard of Oz* classic "Over the Rainbow." McPhee sang simply but with deep feeling. "This is the best vocal of the season for you," Jackson said. Cowell agreed: "That was the single best performance of the competition."

On the next night's results show, the voting was tight. When the news came in that voters had dropped Yamin but left Hicks and McPhee in the race, she was thrilled. After all, McPhee knew, *Idol*'s top two contestants would receive recording contracts.

She didn't have much time for career planning, though. She was heading into the busy week of the championship round.

ALL SHOOK UP: MAY–DECEMBER 2006

During her career's most crucial week, Katherine McPhee was talking loose and easy. "I feel so much freer (than earlier in the competition)," she said about her upcoming sing-off against Taylor Hicks. "We both have record deals now . . . We're both just going to be able to do things that we weren't before *American Idol*."

Hicks and McPhee were different kinds of entertainers. A soul singer from Alabama who had no formal musical training, Hicks had spent years playing in bars and nightclubs. With gray hair and clumsy dance moves, he was an unlikely idol. But his fans, the "Soul Patrol," adored the warm, unpretentious everyman who wrung every drop of gritty emotion from his songs.

McPhee liked Hicks, too. "He definitely knows how to get a crowd going," she said. "If I'd been watching *American Idol*, I probably would've voted for Taylor."

Top Two

On May 23, *American Idol* moved to the 3,400-seat Kodak Theatre in Hollywood. Each performer would do three songs, including two that he or she had already sung on *Idol*.

McPhee sings "Over the Rainbow" on May 23, 2006—the final performance show of *American Idol*'s fifth season.

McPhee opened the show with "Black Horse and the Cherry Tree." The judges liked her work, but Simon Cowell found the bouncy tune too small for such a big night. Later, she launched into "Over the Rainbow." She had agonized over whether to sing it just one week after doing it the first time, but Randy Jackson and Paula Abdul loved her performance, and Cowell called it her best of the season. Finally, she offered "My Destiny," a new ballad about reaching a treasured goal. Abdul loved McPhee's work; Jackson disliked the song; and Cowell felt that after "Over the Rainbow," McPhee had slipped from "brilliant" to only "quite good."

The next night, *Idol* reconvened at the Kodak Theatre for the results show.

The Winner Is . . .

The finale included performances by the season's top dozen contestants, plus videotape highlights of the season. McPhee performed with her fellow contestants and guest star Meat Loaf, a master of powerful arena rock. Toward the end of the show, she sang the joyful romantic ballad "The Time of My Life" with Hicks.

On May 24, the season's final results show, host Ryan Seacrest surprises Katharine McPhee and Taylor Hicks with keys to new cars.

When they finished, Ryan Seacrest came up to them. McPhee and Hicks held hands as Seacrest announced, "Here we go. The winner of *American Idol* Season Five is—Taylor Hicks!"

McPhee and Hicks hugged as the stage lights flashed and the audience roared. Seacrest asked Hicks what he'd like to say to his fans. Hicks howled, "Soul Patrol!" Seacrest asked McPhee the same question. "This was a dream come true," she said. "I'm so, so thrilled to be here."

As Hicks rolled into a big closing number, McPhee quietly left the stage.

Beyond *Idol*

McPhee and Hicks spent the next few days giving interviews to the *Los Angeles Times*, *Entertainment Weekly* magazine, and the TV programs *Access Hollywood*, *Entertainment Tonight*, *Live with Regis and Kelly*, *Larry King Live*, *Today*, and *The Early Show*. The appointments and appearances seemed endless.

Even after the interview flurry faded, McPhee kept making news. On June 6, she signed a record deal with Clive Davis's J Records and *Idol* creator Simon Fuller's music company, 19 Recordings. Three days later, she began a three-show stint with Andrea Bocelli on his concert tour; the two had hit it off so well in April that he invited her to sing with him when his tour hit California. On June 27, 19 Recordings released McPhee's first record—"Over the Rainbow" backed with "My Destiny." Within three weeks, it shot up to number 12 on *Billboard* magazine's sales charts.

At the end of June, McPhee made her biggest news since *Idol*'s finale. *People* magazine hit the stands with "My Secret Struggle," her confession about bulimia. She discussed growing up self-conscious about her body; her treatment at the Eating Disorder Center; and her now-healthy eating habits, which allowed her to drop thirty pounds (about fourteen kilograms) since joining *American Idol*.

McPhee made headlines again a few days later. She had suffered throat problems since *Idol*'s Elvis show, but she had kept singing. Now, *Idol* was about to send its singers on a concert tour: sixty shows in thirty-nine cities over eighty-two days. In rehearsals for the tour, McPhee would finish her first song and find that she couldn't sing another. Just before the tour began on July 5, her doctor diagnosed her with bronchitis and laryngitis. To her disappointment, he put her on three weeks of vocal rest, which meant no singing, no talking, and no touring.

McPhee was finally free to talk on July 26, when she and shampoo maker Sexy Hair Products announced she would appear in the company's advertising. The next day, on the TV talk show *The View*, she not only spoke but also sang "Over the Rainbow."

She joined the *Idol* tour on its July 28 stop in Washington. That night, she performed on the tour for the first time, singing "Over the Rainbow" and "Black Horse and the Cherry Tree." McPhee enjoyed the tour—"one big fun adventure," she said, "like a traveling college campus."

Recording a Record

As the *Idol* tour came to an end, McPhee and her record companies planned her first album. The companies sent her ballads and traditional pop music that was similar to what she had sung on *Idol*, but she preferred more modern, beat-heavy R & B. Frustrated, she turned down a number of songs.

The companies wanted to release the album in November. They needed McPhee to move fast, since albums can take months to make, but she was slowing the entire process.

Finally, when the *Idol* tour ended on September 24, the record companies sent McPhee to Thomas Crown Studios in Virginia Beach, Virginia, home of composer-producer Nate "Danja" Hills. McPhee was delighted. Hills, just two years older than McPhee, had already worked on hit records for Nelly Furtado and Justin Timberlake.

To assemble an album quickly, Hills brought in experts on songwriting for young women. Corte Ellis had written for Beyoncé, and Kara DioGuardi had contributed to hits by Ashlee Simpson, Hilary Duff, and the first *Idol* winner, Kelly Clarkson. Hills, DioGuardi, and Ellis wrote or cowrote seven of the album's twelve songs.

McPhee got to join in writing three of the songs—primarily ones that told men to get lost. The defiant, danceable "Not Ur Girl," for instance, is about breaking off a relationship with a man who had become too attached. The slower, sadder "Neglected" criticizes an ex-boyfriend who had cheated on her.

McPhee spent long days in the studio. She enjoyed singing but said "I was so isolated in the (recording) booth. It was pitch-dark and quiet, and (the producers) would be outside talking, and I'd be like, 'Hello? Guys? What are you saying about me?'" When she did get the producers' attention, she was sometimes timid about challenging them. "I was like, 'I guess this is how it goes. The producer tells you how to sing it, (even) if I don't like it.'" In addition, the album ended up with more ballads than McPhee wanted, and it was finished too late to come out in November. It had to wait until 2007.

Still, McPhee felt that most of the songs had turned out well. And by the end of October, McPhee was back in Los Angeles, enjoying the life of a celebrity.

A Star's Life

By the end of 2006, McPhee had attended the prestigious American Music Awards and Billboard Music Awards; appeared on *The Tonight Show with Jay Leno*; performed at a star-filled charity fund-raiser for diabetes research; done interviews and photo sessions with magazines such as *Shape, Self,* and *Blender;* and crooned "Over the Rainbow" on the CBS special *A Home for the Holidays.* On January 1, 2007, she sang on a flower-covered float in the nationally televised Tournament of Roses parade.

The next day marked the release of the first single off her album. "Over It," which started softly but rose to a passionate

To promote her first album, McPhee appeared on a variety of TV shows. On February 1, 2007, for instance, she cooked with celebrity chef Rachael Ray.

wail, was another get-lost blast. The song quickly became one of the nation's top 30 hits. Its video—in which McPhee found her (fictional) boyfriend betraying her—was an instant hit on MTV's popular *TRL* (*Total Request Live*).

It looked like the girl from Sherman Oaks had a grand future ahead of her.

Chapter 5

COME RAIN OR COME SHINE: THE McPHUTURE

On January 30, 2007, the album *Katharine McPhee* hit record stores. Its cover shocked some people who knew McPhee only as *American Idol*'s sweet, formally gowned angel. Gazing out with a sultry expression, McPhee wore a clingy minidress and held its hem down between her legs, which were spread apart and clad in shiny black boots. She had wanted a more conservative picture, but her record companies overruled her.

The album's reviews were mixed. They ranged from "Great voice . . . but wow, McPhee is working with some poor material" (*Entertainment Weekly*) to "McPhee's debut doesn't render her halfway interesting" (*Rolling Stone*) to "(McPhee) has the makings of a real pop idol" (*People*).

The Publicity Machine

To promote the album, McPhee returned to acting. In mid-January, she played herself on the TV comedy *Ugly Betty*. As a fan of the show, she was nervous on the set at first, but star America Ferrera made her feel welcome. The episode aired on February 1, just two days after her album was released.

With a CD of her album in front of her, McPhee answers questions about her career in March 2007.

Between the filming and the airing of her *Ugly Betty* episode, McPhee appeared in the popular Internet serial "Lonelygirl15." McPhee had followed the series from its start in June 2006. Its video webisodes centered on a naive teenager named Bree and her friends Daniel and Jonas. McPhee filmed the webisode "Truth or Dare" in mid-January, and it hit the Internet on January 19. She played a girl who helped Bree and Jonas handle a drunken Daniel. At one point, "Over It" played in the background.

McPhee also did some modeling. On February 2, Heart Truth—a campaign to warn women about heart disease—hosted the Red Dress Collection, a fund-raising fashion show.

"The hottest moment had to be when sexy singer McPhee stunned the crowd in a teeny, tiny Daniel Swarovski crystal minidress," the *New York Post* reported.

McPhee's publicity caravan rolled on well into the spring. At first, her efforts paid off. *Katharine McPhee* debuted at number 2 in the country and in a week sold 116,000 copies. Six months later, the sales totaled 344,000—not bad, but not huge. Chris Daughtry's first album, by contrast, sold more than 304,000 copies in its first week and after six months hit nearly two million.

Thanks to her fame on *American Idol*, the shampoo company Sexy Hair asked McPhee to star in its advertisements. McPhee and Sexy Hair announced the news at a press conference in New York.

More and More

In May, McPhee's second single hit the radio waves. "Love Story," a joyous burst of club-friendly pop, celebrated falling for a friend.

"Love Story" wasn't as popular as "Over It," but if McPhee was disappointed, she didn't show it. She was busy landing roles in movies. In one of them, she played a member of a sorority that hires a Playboy bunny as its house mother (a live-in manager). She also signed on for *The Last Caller,* a dark and romantic comedy whose producers included Nick Cokas.

McPhee seemed to have a promising future. During her time on *American Idol,* she was asked whose career path she wanted to follow. "I love Barbra Streisand," she answered. "Just look at what she's done. I wouldn't have the same music as her, but she's done everything, and she's been respected with pretty much everything she's done." A moment later, she added, "I want everything any normal person would have—family and kids—but also to have this incredible career."

Glossary

album A long-playing collection of songs or other recorded items.

audition A tryout where a performer shows off his or her abilities.

ballad A slow, usually romantic song.

bingeing Overdoing; for example, overeating.

blues A form of music known for its sorrowful subject matter.

Broadway A theater district in New York City.

bulimia An eating disorder that involves bingeing and purging.

conservatory A school that teaches an art form, usually music.

contestant A person participating in a contest.

episode A part of a series; for instance, an episode of *American Idol.*

lyrics The words of a song.

musical A play in which the characters express themselves by singing and dancing.

pop A form of music known for upbeat rhythms and simple lyrics.

producer The person in charge of making a movie, television show, or record.

purging Getting rid of something; people suffering from bulimia vomit to purge food.

single A record featuring one or two songs.

soul A form of music emphasizing deep, often painful feelings.

For More Information

The Boston Conservatory
8 The Fenway
Boston, MA 02215
Web site: http://www.bostonconservatory.edu
  This college trains students in the fields of music, theater, and dance.

Broadway Theatre Project (BTP)
2780 East Fowler Avenue
Tampa, FL 33612
(888) 874-1764
Web site: http://broadwaytheatreproject.com
  The BTP is a theater program in which students study with professionals
  who are still active in dance, acting, voice, and writing.

FOX Broadcasting Company
P.O. Box 900
Beverly Hills, CA 90213
(310) 369-1000
Web site: http://www.fox.com
  FOX is the television network that airs *American Idol*.

J Records
745 Fifth Avenue, 6th Floor
New York, NY 10151
(646) 840-5600

Web site: http://www.jrecords.com
> J Recordings is a division of RCA Music Group, a unit of Sony BMG, which releases Katharine McPhee's records.

19 Recordings
33 Ransomes Dock
35-37 Parkgate Road
London SW11 4NP
England
(011) 44 20 7801 1919
Web site: http://www.19.co.uk
> 19 Recordings is *American Idol* creator Simon Fuller's record label, which is a sublabel of Universal Records. McPhee makes records for 19 Recordings.

Web Sites

Due to the changing nature of Internet links, Rosen Publishing has developed an online list of Web sites related to the subject of this book. This site is updated regularly. Please use this link to access the list:

http://www.rosenlinks.com/wyi/kamc

For Further Reading

Abramowitz, Rachel. "An Ingenue No Longer: 'American Idol' Runner-Up Katharine McPhee Shows a Sultrier Side on Her New Album." *Los Angeles Times*, January 30, 2007, page E1.

Gershuny, Diane. "Onto the Pot of Gold." *American Idol: The Magazine*, November 2006.

Greenblatt, Leah. "What's on My Mind: Katharine McPhee." *Entertainment Weekly*, January 26, 2007, p. 28.

Halperin, Shirley. "American Beauty." *Teen People*, August 2006, p. 70.

Oldenburg, Ann. "Katharine, Taylor Speak Up." *USA Today*, May 19, 2006, p. D1.

Rizzo, Monica. "Katharine McPhee: The *Idol* Next Door." *People*, February 5, 2007, p. 97.

Seacrest, Ryan. "Interview with Katharine McPhee, Taylor Hicks." *Larry King Live*, May 29, 2006.

Seibel, Deborah Starr. "Katharine McPhee." *TV Guide*, February 5, 2007, p. 26.

Shuster, Fred. "Kat Scratch Fever—Valley Voting Bloc Pulling for its '*Idol*,' Katharine McPhee." *Daily News of Los Angeles*, May 3, 2006, p. U4.

Shuster, Fred. "Sherman Oaks Woman May Be Next *Idol*." *Daily News of Los Angeles*, February 21, 2006, p. N1.

Souter, Ericka. "My Secret Struggle." *People*, July 3, 2006, p. 54.

Tannenbaum, Rob. "Who Does Katharine McPhee Think She Is?" *Blender*, December 2006. Retrieved September 11, 2007 (http://www.blender.com/guide/articles.aspx?id=2210).

Bibliography

Barnes, Ken. "*Idol* Chatter: Candid Commentary on *American Idol* Performances." Retrieved June 25, 2007 (http://blogs.usatoday.com/idolchatter/katharine_mcphee/index.html).

BookRags. "Katharine Hope McPhee." Retrieved July 2, 2007 (http://www.bookrags.com/wiki/Katharine_McPhee).

Fans of Reality TV. "Interview with Katharine McPhee." Retrieved May 30, 2007 (http://www.fansofrealitytv.com/forums/official-articles/54457-american-idol-5-22-06-interview-katharine-mcphee.html).

Getty Images. "Katharine McPhee." Retrieved July 6, 2007 (http://www.gettyimages.com/Search/Search.aspx).

Halperin, Shirley. "American Beauty." *Teen People*, August 2006, p. 70.

Internet Movie DataBase. "*American Idol*: The Search for a Superstar." Retrieved May 22, 2007 (http://www.imdb.com/title/tt0319931).

Internet Movie DataBase. "Katharine McPhee." Retrieved May 1, 2007 (http://www.imdb.com/name/nm1897713).

WireImage. "Katharine McPhee." Retrieved June 17, 2007 (http://www.wireimage.com/SearchResults.aspx?navtyp=SRH&sfld=C&logsrch=1&s=Katharine%20McPhee).

Index

About the Author

David Seidman writes about pop culture. His books include *Adam Sandler, All Gone: Things That Aren't There Anymore,* and adaptations of movies including *King Kong* and *Fantastic Four.* He lives in West Hollywood, California.

Photo Credits

Cover, p. 1 © Getty Images for CineVegas; cover (background photos), pp. 13, 26, 31, 32, 37, 40 © Getty Images; pp. 6, 19, 39 © WireImage/Getty Images; p. 8 © AFP/Getty Images; p. 10 © AP Photos; p. 16 © Ed Krieger; p. 22 © FilMagic/GettyImages.

Designer: Tahara Anderson; **Editor:** Kathy Kuhtz Campbell
Photo Researcher: Marty Levick